Acknowledgement of Land & of the Traditional Owners of this Land

I would like to acknowledge the Gadigal people of the Eora Nation, upon whose stolen land I stand on today.
I recognise that this land was never terra nullius — the land belonging to these peoples was never ceded, given up, bought or sold.
I would like to pay my respects to Aboriginal Elders past, present and emerging, and I extend this acknowledgement to all Aboriginal and Torres Strait Islander people.

CONTENTS

1: There's Blood
(C'è Sangue)
2: The Glass Bead Game
(Il Gioco delle Perle di Vetro)
3: What a Tangled Web We Weave
(Che Ragnatela Intricata Tessiamo)
4: Freak Show
(Spettacolo Strano)
5: **STOP MOLESTING ME!**
(Smettila di Molestarmi!)
6: Life is a Process
(La Vita è un Processo)
7: Sometimes You Just Have a Bad Day
(A Volte Hai Solo una Brutta Giornata)
8: That Was Not My Piss
(though it does possess mystical & magical powers)
(Quello Non era il Mio Piscio (anche se possiede poteri mistici e magici))
9: Journey Through the Past
(Viaggio Nel Passato)
10: Do Nothing
(Fare Niente)
11: **Don't Fuck Around with Mama**
(Non Scopare in Giro con la Mamma)
12: Without Music There Is No Life
(Senza Musica non c'è Vita)
13: **FASCIST UNDERPANTS**
(Mutande Fasciste)
14: A Poetic Life
(Una Vita Poetica)
15: The Walking Dead
(Il Morto che Cammina)
16: Write It Down
(Scrivilo)
17: Do You LO♥E Me?
(Mi Ami?)

CONTENTS

18: **YOU'RE BEING CONTROLLED**
(Sei Controllato)
19: Growth
(Crescita)
20: Wimin
(Donne)
21: (All I can do is) Kiss You Though the Words of a Poem
((Tutto quello che faccio è) Baciarti Anche se lePparole di Una Poesia)
22: How Did I Get Here?
(Come Sono Arrivato Qui?)
23: **THE PUSSY MAFIA**
(La Mafia della Figa)
24: Cosmic Spirituality
(Spiritualità Cosmica)
25: You're Tripping Again!
(Stai di Nuovo Inciampando!)
26: Desolation Road
(Strada della Desolazione)
27: You Gotta Believe in Something
(Devi Credere in Qualcosa)
28: Musical Soul
(Anima Musicale)
29: Don't Let the Music Die
(Non Lasciare che la Musica Muoia)
30: The Work/Living Dilema
(Il Dilema Lavoro/Vivere)
31: Don't Stress
(Non Stressarti)
32: The World of Lost Souls
(Il Mondo delle Anime Perdute)
33: Living is Easy
(don't make it more difficult than it is)
(Vivere è Facile (non renderlo più difficile di quello che è))

CONTENTS

34: Sincerity
(Sincerità)
35: Invasion Day (Australia Day)
(Giorno dell'Invasione (Giornata dell'Australia))
36: She's Been Very Good for Me
(È Stata Molto Brava Con Me)
37: Innocence
(Innocenza)
38: Insecurity
(Insicurezza)
39: Nothing is Set in Stone
(Nulla è Scolpito nella Pietra)
40: Don't Listen to the Words of Fools
(Non Ascoltare le Parole degli Sciocchi)
41: Is This Who I Really Am?
(È Questo Quello che Sono Veramente?)
42: Born Naked, Die Naked
(Nato Nudo, Muori Nudo)
43: Who Gives a Fuck!
(Chi Se ne Frega!)
44: Life is Life
(La Vita è la Vita)
45: Imperfection
(Imperfezione)
46: Coward
(Vigliacco)
47: When Worlds Collide
(Quando i Mondi si Scontrano)
48: No Problemo (It's all good)
(Nessun Problema (Va tutto bene)
49: I'm Not Your Fucking Chauffeur
(Non Sono il tuo Fottuto Autista)
50: Tom Waits' Blues
(Il Blues di Tom Waits)

There's Blood

(C'è Sangue)

There's blood on the *floor*.
There's blood on the *ceiling*.
There's blood on the *walls*.
There's blood on the *carpet*.
There's blood on the *door*.
There's blood on the *windows*.
There's blood on the *ground*.
There's blood on the *dance floor*.
There's blood everywhere.

There's blood in the *sky*.
There's blood in the *water*.
There's blood in the *soil*.
There's blood in the *river*.
There's blood in the *lake*.
There's blood in the *forest*.
There's blood in the *dessert*.
There's blood everywhere.

There's blood on my *hands*
There's blood on my *face*.
There's blood in my *mouth*.
There's blood in my *eyes*.
There's blood in my *hair*.
There's blood in my HE♥RT.
There's blood in my *soul*.
There's blood everywhere.

"I see red, I see red, I see red!"

"I see blood everywhere!"

"The Don"
28.12.2021

The Glass Bead Game

(Il Gioco delle Perle di Vetro)

I feel like I'm in a game.
It's all about strategy.
What's her next move?
She has every move thought out.
She has everything planned.
She's a fantastic strategiser.
Is she playing *"The Glass Bead Game"*?

Has she worked out my game plan?
Does she know what I'm up too?
Can she see my strategy?
Is she onto me already?
She's very good.
In fact, She's the BEST.
At playing...
...*"The Glass Bead Game"*.

She's told me that I'm very good.
The best so far.
That I'm the only one that can keep up with her.
Even match her...
...sometimes.
Now that's high praise...
...I must say.
In fact, I'm flattered.
I must also know how to play...
...*"The Glass Bead Game"*.

"The Don"
29.12.2021

STOP MOLESTING ME!

(Smettila di Molestarmi!)

"Stop molesting me!"
That's what she said.
What's happened to this world...?
...when any signs of affection are considered bad?

STOP MOLESTING ME!

"Don't get too close to me!"
"Don't touch me!"
"Don't hold me!"
"Don't cuddle me!"
"Don't kiss me!"
"And you definitely you can't fuck me!"
Just...

..."STOP MOLESTING ME!"

"Is this LO♥E that I'm feeling?"

"No!"
"You just want to molest me!"

STOP MOLESTING ME!

One person's Lo♥E is another person's molesting.

I can't make any signs of affection...
...because that is molesting!

STOP MOLESTING ME!

"The Don"
03.01.2022

Life is a Process

(La Vita è un Processo)

Enjoy the ride.
Look at the scenery.
Smell the roses.
Watch the sunrise.
Watch the sunset.
Go naked.
Sleep on the sand.
Have adventures.
Be adventurous.
Take risks.
Have FUN.
Make new friends.
Reacquaint yourself with old friends.
Have a siesta.
Breathe.
Listen.
Relax.
Talk.
Tell stories.
Make music.
Sing.
Dance.
Laugh.
Get drunk.
Get stoned.
Get HIGH.
Drop some ACID.
Make LO♥E.
Because...
...life is a process.

"The Don"
03.01.2022

What a Tangled Web We Weave
(Che Ragnatela Intricata Tessiamo)

Confusion.
Delusion.
Twisted paths.
Tortured souls.
Broken HE♥RTS.
Shattered dreams
What a tangled web we weave.

Lies.
Intrigue.
Subterfuge.
Conceit.
Deceit.
Everything is as clear as mud.
What a tangled web we weave.

The path is long & lonely.
There are many hurdles & obstacles along the way.
We do not make it easy for ourselves.
We always take the wrong turn.
We make the wrong decisions.
We become stuck at the *"Crossroads"*.
Which road shall I take?
It's all so confusing.
What a tangled web we weave.

"The Don"
31.12.2021

Freak Show

(Spettacolo Strano)

My life is a *freak show*.
Society is a *freak show*.
The world is a *freak show*.
Life is a *freak show*.
What a *freak show!*

Can you make any sense of this shit?
What the fuck is happening?
What the fuck is going on?
Nothing makes sense.
We're living in a *freak show*.

My life is in turmoil.
Society is in turmoil.
The world is in turmoil.
Governments are in turmoil.
Capitalism is in in turmoil.
Communism is in turmoil.
Socialism is in turmoil.
We're living in a *freak show*.

"The Don"
31.12.2021

Sometimes You Just Have a Bad Day
(A Volte Hai Solo una Brutta Giornata)

This is the human being.
So *complicated*.
So *confused*.
So *misunderstood*.
So *chaotic*.
So *unpredictable*.
So *surprising*.
So *simple*.
But...
...sometimes you just have a bad day!

Life is *sad*.
Life is *good*.
Life is *unpredictable*.
So, take it as it comes.
There's nothing you can do about it
Because…
...sometimes you just have a bad day!

Try to *"live in the moment"*.
Whatever that means.
Try to enjoy your life.
Try to have FUN.
But...
...sometimes you just have a bad day!

And there's nothing you can do about it!

"The Don"
04.01.2022

That Was Not My Piss
(though it does possess mystical & magical powers)
(Quello Non era il Mio Piscio (anche se possiede poteri mistici e magici))

I felt a warm current around my legs.
It started to rise throughout the water.
I immersed myself in the water.
It enveloped me.
I was submersed in its warm embrace.
I surfaced...
...exhilarated.
She looked at me...
...and said...
...that was not my piss.

I feel warm & fuzzy inside.
I feel LO♥E all around.
I feel light-headed.
I feel HIGH.
"I think you're tripping!"
Because....
...that was not my piss.

I see colours in the sky.
I see beauty everywhere...
...and in everything.
...and in everyone.
"Don't say that I'm just tripping."
"Ok!"
"Maybe..."
"......it was my piss!"

"It does have mystical & magical powers!"

"The Don" + Miriam
04.01.2022

Journey Through the Past
(Viaggio Nel Passato)

I remember when I was young.
Of times when I was free.
Of good times had with my friends.
They were good times.
Of complete abandonment.
Making music in my friend's old garage.
All night long.
From sunset.
Until sunrise.
All night long.
Singing.
Laughing.
Getting *STONED*.
Getting *HIGH*.
Dropping *ACID*.
Searching for the *"Meaning of Life"*.
But finding no answers.
Still, it didn't stop us.
Because we'd do again…
…many times over.
I still carry those days with me.
Inside of me.
They were definitely good times.

"The Don"
04.12.2022

Do Nothing

(Fare Niente)

Do nothing.
It's as simple as that.
Do nothing.
That's all you have to do.
Do nothing.
Let the Universe do its thing.
Do nothing.
Let events unfold by themselves.
Do nothing.
Just be.
Do nothing.
And everything will happen.
Do nothing.
That's the key.
Do nothing.
Just let it be.
Do nothing.
You will set yourself free.
Do nothing.
And everything will come to thee.
Do nothing.
It's as simple as that.
Do nothing.
It couldn't be any easier.
Do nothing.
And just enjoy the ride.
Do nothing.
You are taking part in an adventure.
Do nothing.
Just wait & see.
Do nothing.
And set yourself free.
Do nothing.
Make no demands.
Do nothing.
Let her make the moves.
Do nothing.

"The Don"
05.01.2022

Don't Fuck Around with Mama

(Non Scopare in Giro con la Mamma)

She knows her game.
She's number one.
She's the BEST.
So...
...don't fuck around with mama.

You wanna take her on?
Do you think you're up to it?
Do you have the power?
Do you have the mental strength?
Because if you don't...
Then...
...don't fuck around with mama.
Because...
...you're gonna lose!

She's a *"Force to be reckoned with"*.
She's a *"Force of Nature"*.
She's got *"Girl Power"*!
She's a *"Brazilian Gatinha"*
She's an *"Amazonian Warrior"*!
So...
...don't fuck around with mama.
...you're gonna lose!

So...
"...come to mama!"
"...and let's party!"
"Are you up for it?"

"The Don"
04.01.2022

Without Music There Is No Life

(Senza Musica non c'è Vita)

Make sure you *have music inside you*.
Make sure you *feel the music inside you*.
Make sure you *listen to the music inside you*.
Make sure you *hear the music inside you*.
Because...
...*without music there is no life*.

Music is *everywhere*.
Music is in the *air*.
Music is in the *wind*.
Music in the *sunlight*.
Music is in the *moonlight*.
Music is inside you.
Because...
...*without music there is no life*.

See music.
Breathe music.
Hear music.
Feel music.
Live music.
Because...
...*without music there is no life*.

"The Don"
07.01.2022

FASCIST UNDERPANTS

(Mutande Fasciste)

I don't like *to be controlled in this way*.
I don't like *being manipulated*.
I don't like *being forced to do things*.
I don't like wearing *"Fascist underpants"!*

WTF!
"Monday underpants" must be worn ONLY on Mondays!
"Tuesday underpants" must be worn ONLY on Tuesdays!
I can't *do this!*
I can't *live this way.*
I do not want to he controlled by my underpants.
I don't like wearing *"Fascist underpants"!*

"Oh FUCK!"
"Where's "Wednesday"?"
"Holy shit..."
"...I've lost "Wednesday"!"
"Can I wear "Thursday" instead?"
"Is it allowed?"
"I'd better not!"
"I'll go "cammando" instead."
Better to be safe than sorry.
The *"Underpants Gestapo"* might catch me.
I don't like wearing *"Fascist underpants"!*

"Shit..."
"...I hope nobody heard me!"
"Can they read my thoughts?"

"The Don"
09.01.2022

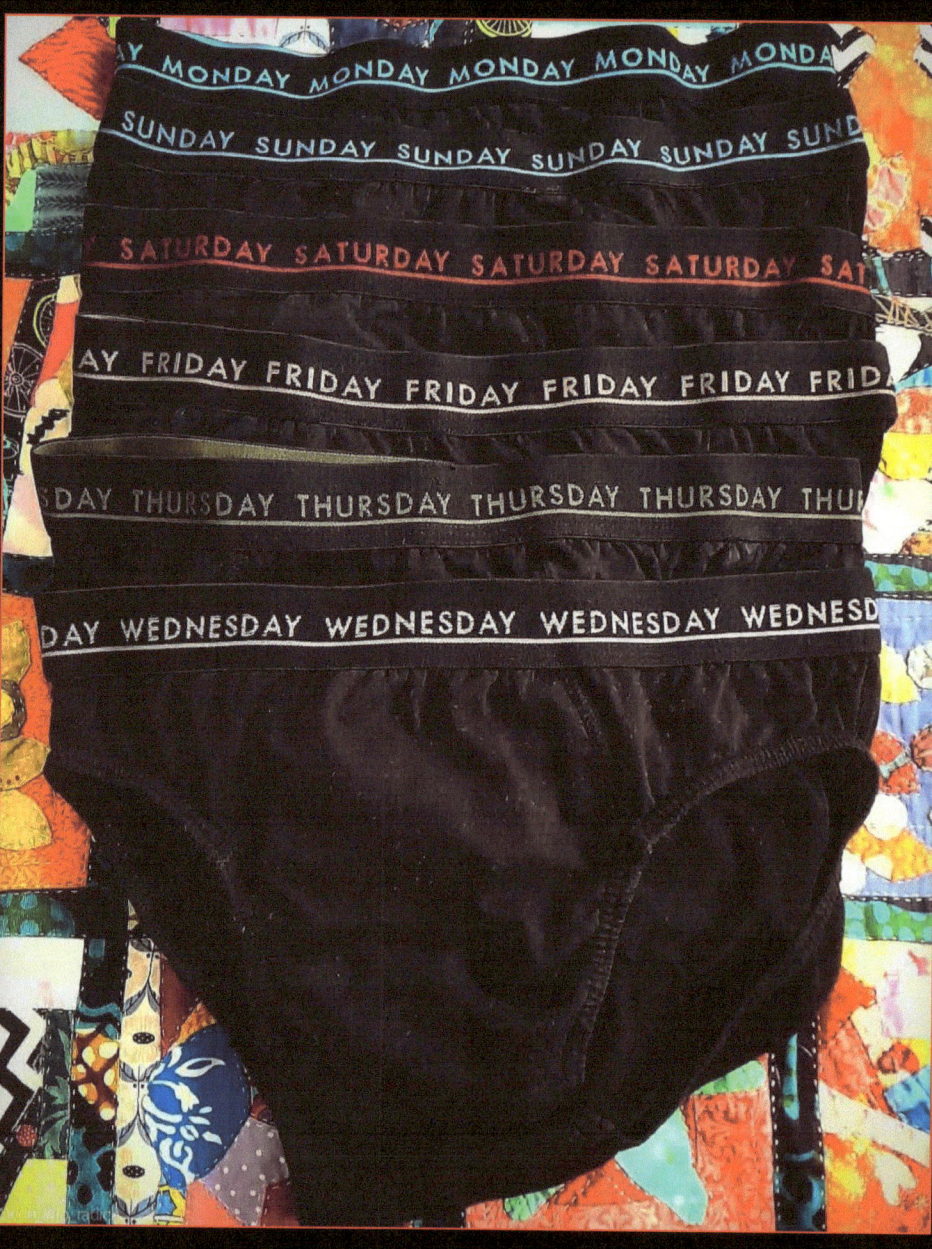

A Poetic Life

(Una Vita Poetica)

To *see what you have to see.*
To *hear what you have to hear.*
To *think what you have to think.*
To *imagine what you have to imagine.*
To *dream what you have to dream.*
To *feel what you have to feel.*
To *experience what you have to experience.*
To *pleasure what you have to pleasure.*
To *LO❤E what you have to LO❤E.*
To *Be what you have to Be.*
To *LIVE what you have to LIVE.*
To *create what you have to create.*
To *live a "Poetic Life".*

Nothing else *is important.*
Nothing else *matters.*
Nothing else *exists.*
Only *"The Moment"* exists.
This is to live a *"Poetic Life".*

"The Don"
11.01.2022

The Walking Dead

(Il Morto che Cammina)

We've removed their *anonymity*.
We've removed their *autonomy*.
We've removed their *individuality*.
We've removed their *personality*.
We've removed their *creativity*.
We've removed their *imagination*.
We've removed their *identity*.
We've removed their *mind*.
We've removed their *thoughts*
We've removed their *dreams*.
We've removed their *brain*.
We've removed their *power*.
We've removed their *dignity*.
We've removed their *humanity*.
We've removed their *soul*.

We have total control.
They have nothing left.
They are completely empty.
They are the *"Walking Dead"*!

(Scrivilo)

Write *down...*
...your *feelings.*
...your *emotions.*
...your *thoughts.*
...your *fears.*
...your *struggles.*
...your *pain.*
...your *suffering.*
...your *ideas.*
...your *dreams.*
...your *nightmares.*
...your *illusions.*
...your *delusions.*
...your *rejections.*
...your *failures.*
...your *successes.*
...your *happiness.*
...your *LO♥ES*
...your *hatreds*

Write it all down.
Don't keep them inside.
Don't keep them bottled up inside you to fester.
Let them out.
Tell the world.
Let the world know who you are.
Let the world know what's inside you.
Write it down.

"The Don"
12.01.2022

Do You LO♥E Me?
(Mi Ami?)

Do You LO♥E Me?
Not as much as you LO♥E Me!

"The Don"
13.01.2022

YOU'RE BEING CONTROLLED

(Sei Controllato)

You're being *manipulated*.
You're being *told what to do*.
You're being *led*.
You're being *fed*.
You're being *duped*.
You're being *doped*.
You're being *dumbed down*.
You're being *told lies*.
You're being *brainwashed*.
You're being *"Zombified"*.
You're being *confined*.
You're being *disempowered*.
You're being *defined*.
You're being *"atomised"*.
You're being *objectified*.
You're being *dehumanised*.
You're being controlled!

"The Don"
14.01.2022

Growth

(Crescita)

Everything grows.
Plants grow.
Animals grow.
The Universe is growing.
Humans grow.
You can grow...
...if you want to.

Let yourself experience growth.
It's easy to do.
Just *"let go"!*
That's all you have to do.
Abandon your fears.
Relinquish your burden.
Be free.
And growth will happen.

Growth is the natural order of things.
Don't *stop it.*
Don't *hinder it.*
Don't *impede it.*
Don't *fight it.*
Accept growth.

It's *evolution.*
It's the *"Universe".*
It's the *"Life Process".*
It's what you have to do.
It's what you MUST do.
There is no alternative.
It's either growth...
...or DEATH!

I choose growth!

"The Don"
14.01.2022

(All I can do is) Kiss You Though the Words of a Poem
((Tutto quello che faccio è) Baciarti Anche se lePparole di Una Poesia)

You don't want me...
...I know that.
But that doesn't stop what I feel inside.
It doesn't placate it.
It doesn't quench my thirst.
It doesn't put out the fire in my belly.
It doesn't stop the butterflies in my stomach.
It doesn't make it easier for me to breathe.
I doesn't give me new eyes so I can see again.
So, all I can do...
...is kiss you through words of a poem.

"The Don"
16.01.2022

Wimin

(Donne)

Fuck men!
We don't need them.
And we certainly don't need them to define us.
And especially in our name.
From now on we are no longer *"women"*...
...we are *"Wimin"!*
We are *"Winners"!*

It's all about empowerment.
Let's take back our power.
Let's assume our power.
We are now *"wimin"!*
We have reclaimed our power.

We are *"wimin"*.
We have the power.
We don't need fucking men.
They have kept as slaves for millennia.
We are "Wimin".

Fuck men.
We don't need them.
They need us but we don't need them.
We can satisfy ourselves in every way.
Physically, psychologically & emotionally.
Men, know your place...
...beneath our feet!
We are "Wimin"!
We have the power.
"Wimin" power!

"The Don" & Miriam
14.01.2022

How Did I Get Here?
(Come Sono Arrivato Qui?)

You may ask yourself?
"How did I get here?"
And you may ask yourself?
"Who am I?"
And you may ask yourself?
"Who are you?"
And you may ask yourself?
"Why am I here?"
And you may ask yourself?
"Where am I going?"
And you may ask yourself?
"What am I supposed to do?"
And you may ask yourself?
"Am I alone?"
And you may ask yourself?
"Are you here to help me?"
And you may ask yourself?
"What is this all about?"
And you may ask yourself?
"Is this just a dream that I'm having?"
And you may ask yourself?
"Or is this a nightmare?"
And you may ask yourself?

And you may ask yourself?

And you may ask yourself?

And you may ask yourself?

"The Don"
16.01.2022

THE PUSSY MAFIA

(La Mafia della Figa)

The *"Pussy Mafia"* is in action.
It knows what it wants.
And it knows how to get it.
Put the **"PUSSY MAFIA"** into action.

Barries to be broken.
My eyes wide open.
Lies to destroy.
The **"PUSSY MAFIA"** is your "realistic" solution.

Do you have any problems that need to be sorted out?
Men problems?
Money issues?
Bureaucracy headaches?
Work related situation?
Whatever it is.
Let the **"PUSSY MAFIA"** sort it out.

Discretion guaranteed.
Results guaranteed.
Satisfaction guaranteed.
With very little fuss.
No dramas.
So, let the **"PUSSY MAFIA"** help you out.

Our motto:
"Come to mamma!"
"THE PUSSY MAFIA".

"The Don" + Miriam
14.01.2022

Cosmic Spirituality

(Spiritualità Cosmica)

It's not the *worship of objects or deities*.
It's not the *belief in supernatural powers*.
It's not the *belief supernatural beings*.
It's the understanding of the Universe & our place within it.
This is "Cosmic Spirituality".

It's an understanding if oneself & our connection with everything around us.
It's the understanding that we are all connected with each other & the Universe.
It's the understanding that we are *"interconnected"*
That we are part of a *"Whole"*.
That we are all part *"One"*.
That there is *no separation.*
That we are *not individuals.*
But rather, that we are *"One"*.
One *"Being"*.
One *"Soul"*.
One *"Entity"*.
This is "Cosmic Spirituality".

"The Don"
17.01.2022

You're Tripping Again!

(Stai di Nuovo Inciampando!)

That's what I want...
...that doesn't mean it's going to happen.
And probably not.
Stop...
...you're tripping again!

Come back down to Earth.
Take a grip on yourself.
Come back to *"Reality"*!
You're tripping again!

When you're sitting back enjoying a *"joint"*.
And start thinking about your favourite girl/boy...
...or whatever your predilection.
And that she's gonna *"Insta"* you.
Creating fantasy scenarios in your head that you know will never happen.
Stop!
You're tripping again!

You're just...
...tripping again.!

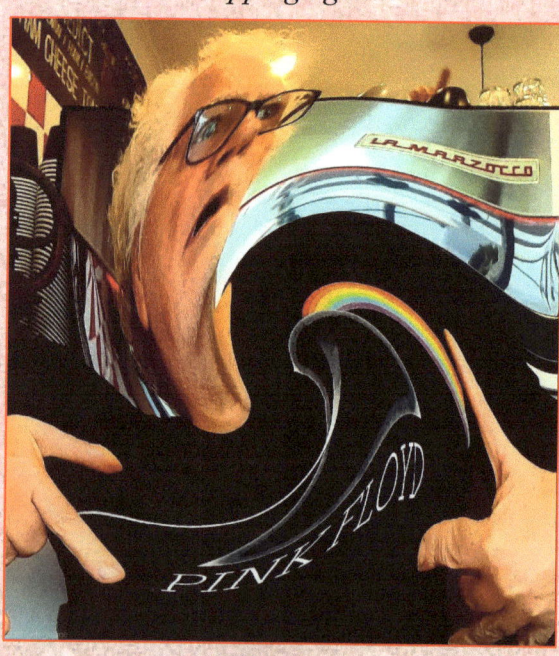

"The Don"
17.01.2022

Desolation Road

(Strada della Desolazione)

You're walking down that *road*.
You're walking down that *highway*.
That highway that *you know the best*.
It could be *"Highway 61"*.
It could be the *"Broken Highway"*.
It could be *"Copperhead Head Road"*.
It could be *"Abby Road"*.
It could be the *"Road to Timbuktu"*.
It could be *"Ventura Highway"*.
It could be the *"Telegraph Road"*.
It could be the *"Yellow Brick Road"*.
It could be *"Thunder Road"*.
It could be the *"Long & Winding Road"*.
It could be a *"Dirt Road"*.
It could be the *"Silk Road"*.
It could be the *"Lost Highway"*.
It could be *"Highway Star"*.
It could be the *"Highway to Hell"*.
It could be a *"Road to Nowhere"!*

But make sure it's not "Desolation Road"!

"The Don"
17.01.2022

You Gotta Believe in Something
(Devi Credere in Qualcosa)

And the *"Universe"* is the best thing that I've come up with.
It's better than most of other things.
Better than *God*.
Better than *mysticism*.
Better than the *supernatural*.
Better than the *occult*.
Better than *spirituality*.
Better than *religion*.
Better than *materialism*.
Better than *Consumerism*.
Better than *Capitalism*.
Better than *"Communism"*.
Better than *"Socialism"*.
Better than *politics*.
Better than *a career*.
Better than *family*.
Better than *"Individuality"*.
Better than *"Nihilism"*.
Better than *"Existentialism.*

"The Don"
18.01.2022

Musical Soul

(Anima Musicale)

Maybe you can hear music.
But can you feel music?
Can you feel it in your *HE♥RT?*
Can you feel it in your *BEING?*
Can you feel it in your *Soul?*
Do you have a "Musical Soul"?

Do you let the music *wash over you?*
Do you let the music *envelope you?*
Do you let the music *enter you?*
Do you let the music *fill you?*
Do you let the music *take over you?*
Do you let the music *enter your HE♥RT?*
Do you let the music *enter your BEING?*
Do you let the music *enter your Soul?*
Do you have a "Musical Soul"?

Let the music *wash over you.*
Let the music *envelope you.*
Let the music *enter you.*
Let the music *fill you.*
Let the music *take over you.*
Let the music *enter your HE♥RT.*
Let the music *enter you being.*
Let the music *enter your Soul.*
If you do...
...you will have a "Musical Soul".

"The Don"
20.01.2022

Don't Let the Music Die
(Non Lasciare che la Musica Muoia)

When *"Don McLean"* sang.
"The day the music died!",
It didn't really die.
It only died for him.
The music kept playing.
It's that he just couldn't hear it anymore.
He had lost his ears.
He could no longer hear it.
He could not feel it any more.
He could no longer feel.
He had lost his HE♥RT.
He had lost it.
He had lost the music.
The music had died for him.
Don't let the music die...
...for you.
...inside you.

Don't let the music die!

"The Don"
20.01.2022

The Work/Living Dilema

(Il Dilema Lavoro/Vivere)

I work.
You work.
We all work.
Why?
To make money!
But...
...*don't live to work*.
Work to live!

Don't let work *control you*.
Don't let work *consume you*.
Don't let work *define you*.
Don't let work *be your LIFE*.
Don't live to work.
Work to live!

Don't be a slave to *work*.
Don't be a slave to *money*.
Don't be a slave to *corporate greed*.
Don't be a slave to *profit*.
Don't be a slave to *exploitation*.
Don't be a slave to *Capitalism*.
Don't be a slave to *the System*.
Don't be a slave to *the Establishment*.
Don't live to work!

Don't sell *yourself*.
Don't sell your *life*.
Don't sell your *happiness*.
Don't sell your *HE❤RT*.
Don't sell your *Soul*.
Don't sell your *Being*.
Don't live to work.
Work to live!

Work to live!

Work to live!

Work to live!

Work to live!

"The Don"
20.01.2022

Don't Stress

(Non Stressarti)

Don't stress over things you can't control.
There is not much that you can control anyway.
So, there is not much to stress about.
So, don't stress.

Even the very few things that you can control...
...don't stress.
That's not to say that you shouldn't plan or be concerned about things.
It just means...
...don't stress.

"Don't sweat the small stuff!"
Look at the big picture.
Change your *perspective*.
Change your "point of view".
Change your *glasses*.
Change your *"mindset"*.
So that you...
...don't stress.

Prioritise.
Rationalise.
Downsize.
Simplify.
Harmonise.
Equilibrate.
Humanise.
So that you...
...don't stress.

Just...
...don't stress.

"The Don"
21.01.2022

The World of Lost Souls

(Il Mondo delle Anime Perdute)

Wandering *aimless*.
With no *direction*.
With no *destination*.
With no *aim*.
With no *purpose*.
With no *meaning*.
With no *LIFE*.
I'm living in *the "World of Lost Souls"*.

How did *this happen?*
How did *it become like this?*
How did *this place become a cemetery?*
How did it *become a lifeless world?*
How did it *lose its humanity?*
How did it become...
...the *"World of Lost Souls"*?

I don't belong here.
I want to get out of here.
I want to escape this barren place.
I want to run away from this *"Dead World"*.
I want to leave...
...the *"World of Lost Souls"*.

"The Don"
21.01.2022

Living is Easy

(don't make it more difficult than it is)
(Vivere è Facile (non renderlo più difficile di quello che è))

Living is easy.
Don't make it more difficult than it is.
By...
Over thinking.
Stressing out.
Panicking.
Freaking out.
Getting angry.
Getting annoyed.
Losing it.
Losing *focus*.
Losing your *mind*.
Losing your *"religion"*.
Losing your HE❤RT.
Losing your *Soul*.
Losing you *Being*.
Losing your *identity*.
Being *negative*.
Being *pessimistic*.
Being *worried*.
Seeing the glass *"half-full"*.
Seeing *"red"*.
Seeing the *"writing on the wall"*.
Becoming *disheartened*.
Living is easy (don't make it more difficult than it is).

"The Don"
22.01.2022

Sincerity

(Sincerità)

All I want is Sincerity.
Sincerity is *simple*.
Sincerity is *from the HE*❤️*RT*.
Sincerity is *kindness*.
Sincerity is *compassion*.
Sincerity is *friendship*.
Sincerity is *consideration*.
Sincerity is *understanding*.
Sincerity is *connection*.
Sincerity is *caring*.
Sincerity is *kindness*.
Sincerity is *egoless*.
Sincerity is *respect*.
Sincerity is *simplicity*.
Sincerity is *oneness*.
Sincerity is *openness*.
Sincerity is *inner beauty*.
Sincerity is *unity*.
Sincerity is *humanity*.
Sincerity is *LO*❤️*E*.
All I want is sincerity.

"The Don" + Miriam
23.01.2022

Invasion Day (Australia Day)

(Giorno dell'Invasione (Giornata dell'Australia))

It's celebrated.
It's celebrated as *"Australia day"*.
It's a *"White Man"* celebration.
It's a public holiday.
There are fireworks on the harbour.
There is fire in the sky.
The sky is on fire.
It is raining tears of flames.
The Universe is burning on this day.
It is a day to cry.
It is a day of shame.
For *"First Nations Peoples"*, it is NOT a day to celebrate.
It is a day to mourn.
It is a day of anger.
It is "Invasion Day"!

On the 26th January 1778.
Captain Arthur Phillip landed on the shore of *"Port Jackson"*.
With 12 ships called *"The First Fleet"*.
These ships carried convicts from England.
He claimed this land for the *"British Empire"*!
It was not his to claim.
The land was already own by *"First Nations Peoples"*.
It was an invasion!
It was "Invasion Day"!

Australia was set up as a *"penal colony"* of the British Empire.
White man stole the land.
White man destroyed, plundered, raped, pillaged & killed *"First Nations Peoples"!*
A spear & a boomerang is no match for a musket & gunpowder.
This day is not a day to celebrate.
This day is a day to cry.
This day is a day of shame.
This day is "Invasion Day"!

It is "Invasion Day"!

Let us *not distort history*.
Let us *not rewrite history*.
Let us *know the truth*.
Let us *face the truth*.
Let us *face the grim horror of that day*.
Of the atrocities that were carried out.
What are we celebrating?
Why are we celebrating...?
..."Invasion Day"!

There is *blood in the water*.
There is *blood in the land*.
There is *blood on in the sky*.
There is *blood on your hands*.
There is *blood in your HE♥RT*.
There is *blood in your SOUL*.
There is *blood everywhere*.
The sky is crying blood.

"Australia Day" is "Invasion Day"!

Not a day celebrate!

It's a day to cry!

"Australia Day" is "Invasion Day"!

"The Don"
25.01.2022

She's Been Very Good for Me
(È Stata Molto Brava Con Me)

I've learnt a lot.
She's taught me a lot.
It's been quite a ride.
It's been quite an adventure.
She's been very good for me.

It's been a *musical journey*.
It's been a *cultural adventure*.
It's been a *philosophical quest*.
It's been an *emotional roller-coaster*.
She's been very good for me.

I don't know *where we are going*.
I don't know *how this will end*.
I don't know *if it will end*.
I don't *have a clue what's going on*.
The only thing I know for certain is...
...she's been very good for me.

And I think I've been very good for her.

"The Don"
27.01.2022

Innocence

(Innocenza)

Innocence is being *"wide-eyed"*.
Innocence is being *curious*.
Innocence is being *adventurous*.
Innocence is being a *risk-taker*.
Innocence is being *unpredictable*.
Innocence is being *spontaneous*
Innocence is being *fun lo♥ing*.
Innocence is being *crazy*.
Innocence is being *funny*.
Innocence is being *happy*.
Innocence is being *care-free*.
Innocence is being *positive*.
Innocence is being *"open-minded"*.
Innocence is being *unconventional*.
Innocence is being *"light"*.
Innocence is being *one with the "Universe"*.
Innocence is taking *chances*.
Innocence is *LO♥E*.
I LO♥E innocence.

Innocence is *not taking yourself seriously*.
Innocence is *having no prejudices*.
Innocence is *allowing people to be whomever they want to be*.
Innocence is *having no fear*.
Innocence is *beautiful*.
Innocence is *LO♥ING without limits*.
Innocence is *LO♥ING everyone*.
Innocence is *having an open HE♥RT*.
Innocence is *being humane*.
Innocence is *being human*.
I LO♥E innocence.

NEVER lose your innocence!

"The Don"
27.01.2022

Insecurity

(Insicurezza)

Doubt.
Jealousy.
Fear.
Uncertainty.
Questioning.
Faith.
Trust.
Possessiveness.
Ownership.
Control.
Power.
It's just insecurity.

Will she message me?
Does she ever think of me?
Do I mean anything to her at all?
Does she LO❤E me?
Will she EVER LO❤E me?
I am full of doubt.
It's just insecurity.

Insecurity is a SHIT!
It creates a hole in your gut.
Let it go.
And replace it with positivity.
Fill the hole with self-worth.
Be FREE.
Live LIFE.
Don't let insecurity control you.
Don't let insecurity rule your life.
Get rid of...
...insecurity!

And be happy!
Have FUN!
Remember...
...it's just insecurity.

"The Don"
28.01.2022

Nothing is Set in Stone
(Nulla è Scolpito nella Pietra)

Don't fear *change*.
Don't fear *the future*.
Don't fear *the unknown*.
Don't fear *anything*.
Because...
...*nothing is set in stone.*

Nothing is *certain*.
Nothing is *determined*.
Nothing is *predetermined*.
Nothing is *preordained*.
Nothing is *destined*.
Nothing is *fate*.
Nothing is set in stone.

Be *free*.
Be *adventurous*.
Be *ridiculous*.
Be *weird*.
Be *funny*.
Be *unconventional*.
Be *crazy*.
Be *spontaneous*.
Be *wild*.
Because...
...*nothing is set in stone.*

Take *chances*.
Take *risks*.
Take the *backroads*.
Take the *wild side*.
Take the *road less travelled*.
Take the *side alleys*.
Take the *dirt path*.
Because...
...*nothing is set in stone.*

Define yourself!

"The Don"
28.01.2022

Don't Listen to the Words of Fools

(Non Ascoltare le Parole degli Sciocchi)

Don't listen to your *parents*.
Don't listen to *priests*.
Don't listen to *politicians*.
Don't listen to *lawyers*.
Don't listen to *economists*.
Don't listen to *"experts"*.
Don't listen to *"warmongers"*.
Don't listen to *"peacemakers"*.
Don't listen to the *DEVIL*.
Don't listen to *GOD*
Don't listen to *me*.
Don't listen to the words of fools.

Don't listen to *celebrities*.
Don't listen to *psychologists*.
Don't listen to *intellectuals*.
Don't listen to the *church*.
Don't listen to *religions*.
Don't listen to *gurus*.
Don't listen to *leaders*.
Don't listen to *psychopaths*.
Don't listen to *governments*.
Don't listen to *Capitalists*.
Don't listen to *Socialist*.
Don't listen to *Communists*.
Don't listen to *aristocrats*.
Don't listen to the words of fools.

"The Don"
29.01.2022

Is This Who I Really Am?
(È Questo Quello che Sono Veramente?)

Is this who I really am?
Is this who I really am?
Is this who I really am?
Is this who I really am?
Is this who I really am?
Who the fuck am I?
Is this who I really am?

I don't know who the fuck I am.
I have no idea who the fuck I am.
Who the fuck am I?
Is this who I really am?

What the fuck!
Who the fuck am I?
I have no fucking idea who I am?
Who the fuck am I, really?
Is this who I really am?

Is this who I really am?

Is this who the fuck I really am?

Is this who I really am?

Is this who I really am?

"The Don"
29.01.2022

Born Naked, Die Naked

(Nato Nudo, Muori Nudo)

We are *all just visitors on this planet.*
We are *not here to stay.*
We are *only passing through.*
We *are just on a journey...*
...a journey called *"LIFE".*
You can't take anything with you.
You are born naked & you die naked.

There is no point *accumulating all those material objects.*
There is no point *amassing money.*
There is no point in being *greedy.*
There is no point in *ownership.*
You can't take anything with you.
You are born naked & you die naked.

Dispose.
Divest.
Unburden.
Become *naked.*
Become *free.*
Become *happy.*
You can't take anything with you.
You are born naked & you die naked.

You can't take it with you!
You are born naked & you die naked!

"The Don"
31.01.2022

Who Gives a Fuck!

(Chi Se ne Frega!)

It doesn't matter.
It's all good.
Everything will work out...
...in the end.
And if it doesn't...
...it's NOT the end yet!
So why FREAK out?
Why STRESS out?
Why PANIC?
let it all go!
Because...
...*who gives a FUCK!*

What will be, will be.
There is only so such much you can do.
There is only so much that you can control
There is only so much you have control over.
And that is...
...NOT much!
So don't worry!
Relax.
Breathe.
Have a *drink.*
Have a *joint.*
Have a *laugh.*
Actually, *laugh a lot!*
This is the best medicine...
...*breathe.*
...*drink.*
...*smoke a joint.*
...*laugh.*
Because...
...*who gives a FUCK!*

"The Don"
31.01.2022

Life is Life

(La Vita è la Vita)

Life is *unpredictable*.
Life is *chaotic*.
Life is *uncontrollable*.
Life is *random*.
Life is *accidental*.
Life is *surprising*.
Life is *depressing*.
Life is *wonderful*.
Life is *beautiful*.
Life is *disorderly*.
Life is *orderly*.
Life is *euphoric*.
Life is *terrible*.
Life is *ugly*.
Life is *unjust*.
Life is *unfair*.
Life is *easy*.
Life is *hard*.
Life is *sad*.
Life is *happy*.
Life is *ridiculous*.
Life is *hilarious*.
Life is *tragic*.
Life is *funny*.
Life is *strange*.
Life is *competitive*.
Life is *illogical*.
Life is *logical*.
Life is *simple*.
Life is *awesome*.
Life is *codified*.
Life is *structured*.
Life is *unstructured*.

Life is *nonsensical*.
Life is *complicated*.
Life is *uncomplicated*.
Life is *heavy*.
Life is *light*
Life is *hopeless*.
Life is *horrible*.
Life is *horrendous*.
Life is *hideous*.
Life is *utopian*.
Life is *Hell*.
Life is *Heaven*.
Life is *LO♥ING*.
Life is *HATING*.
Life is life!

"The Don"
31.01.2022

Imperfection

(Imperfezione)

Imperfection is perfection.
It's a light into the *indoors*.
It's a light into the *darkness*.
Or into the *light*.
Work it out!
It's a code...
...if you want it to be?
Imperfection is everywhere.
Imperfection is in all of us.
Nothing is perfect.
If you want to achieve perfection, be aware you are not nature.
You are human!
And humans are *imperfect!*
Accept your *imperfections*.
Accept yourself.

Perfection most of the time can lead you to deception.
What do you want from me anyway?
I can speak & act anyway I want.
I can do...
...and not do...
... anything I want.
Because...
...*I'm imperfect*.

I never offered you *perfection*.
I can only give you...
...*imperfection*.

"The Don" + Miriam
31.01.2022

Coward

(Vigliacco)

You're a coward!
You're riddled with a cancer.
It's *spreading throughout your entire body.*
It's *consuming you from the inside.*
It's *eating you up.*
It's *terminal.*
It's *fatal.*
There is NO cure.
It's called *"FEAR"!*

You're a coward!
You're *full of "FEAR"!*
You're *too scared to confront it.*
You're *held tight in its grip.*
It has you by the *"balls"...*
...and, it's not letting go.

You're a coward!
You're *weak.*
You're *pathetic.*
You're *grovelling.*
You're *pleading…*
...*"Not me!"*
...*"Not me!"*
...*"Please God, not me!"*

You're a coward!
Be *strong.*
Put up a *struggle.*
Put up a *fight.*
Put up some *"resistance".*
Be a *"warrior".*
Be a *"fighter".*
Be a "survivor"
Don't be a coward all your life!

Stand up to it.
Don't let *"FEAR" control you.*
Don't let *"FEAR" destroy you.*
Don't let *"FEAR" win.*
Don't let *"FEAR" kill you.*
Don't be a coward!

"The Don"- 01.02.2022

When Worlds Collide

(Quando i Mondi si Scontrano)

When worlds collide.
Expect the unexpected.
Anything can happen.
All your *"hidden"* secrets will be revealed.
All you *"dirty laundry"* will be hung up to dry.
For everything that you are.
You will be exposed.
Everyone will see the *"real"* you...
...and realise that you are a...
...*FAKE!*

When worlds collide.
Everything is laid out on the table.
You will have no place to hide.
No place to run to.
You will become immobilised.
Like a kangaroo caught in the headlights of a car.
You will be a be to see the crash coming...
...but you are powerlessness to stop it.
Transfixed by its gravitational force.
Held to its tragic fate...
...*tragic for you!*

When worlds collide.
There is nothing you can do.
You know that there is going to be damage.
You just hope that the damage won't be too great.
That it will be manageable.
That you will survive it.
That you will not be mortally wounded.
And that you'll come out of it relatively unscathed.
And the damage can be repaired.
You hope!
When worlds collide.

"The Don"
01.02.2022

No Problemo (It's all good)

(Nessun Problema (Va tutto bene)

No problem.
It's all good.
No worries.
Relax.
It is what it is.
Don't worry.
It'll all work out.
Keep calm.
"Calma".
Take it easy.
Don't fret.
Everything's fine.
There's nothing you can do about it.
Nothing at all.
So just let it go.
Move on.
Forget about it.
Fuck it all.
That's LIFE!
It's life & life only.
It's not a problem.
Who gives a fuck anyway?
FUCK it!
That's the way it is.
You can't do anything about it.
So just FUCK it.
Let her go.
It's not a problem.
It's all good.

FUCK it all!

"The Don"
02.02.2022

I'm Not Your Fucking Chauffeur

(Non Sono il tuo Fottuto Autista)

I'm not your *"cuckold"*.
I'm not you *"gopher"*
I'm not your *"lackey"*.
I'm not your *"come here boy"*.
I'm not your *"man-servant"*.
I'm not your *"plaything"*.
I'm not your *"clown"*.
I'm not your *"toy"*.
I'm not your *"slave"*.
I'm not your *"patsy"*.
I'm not your *"errand boy"*.
I'm not your *"puppet"*.
I'm not your *"pin cushion"*.
I'm not your *"after-thought"*.
I'm not your *"whipping boy"*.
I'm not your *"backstop"*.
I'm not your *"whenever guy"*.
I'm not your *"commodity"*.
I'm not your *"poet"*.
I'm not your *"driver"*...
...*to drive you to your next fuck!*

I'm not your FUCKING chauffeur!

"The Don"
02.02.2022

Tom Waits' Blues

(Il Blues di Tom Waits)

He has a really deep, raspy, gravelly voice.
He sounds like he's swallowed razorblades.
He can sing anything.
But he can sing the blues better than "Blind Willie McTell"!

He can sing *folk songs*.
He can sing *jazz songs*.
He can sing *vaudeville songs*.
He can sing *sea-shanti songs*.
He can sing *punk songs*.
He can sing *LO♥E songs*.
But he can sing the blues better than "Blind Willie McTell"!

He is *"butt"* ugly.
He wears old clothes.
He looks like a hobo.
He looks like he hasn't slept for weeks.
He likes to drink a lot.
He likes to smoke, a lot!
But he can sing the blues better than "Blind Willie McTell"!

He sings about *loneliness*.
He sings about *sadness*.
He sings about *loss*.
He sings about *tragedy*.
He sings about *LO♥E*.
He sings about *unrequited LO♥E*.
But he can sing about the blues better than "Blind Willie McTell"!

"The Don"
03.02.2022

Books written by "The Don"

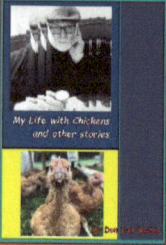
"My Life with Chickens & other stories: I Pity the Poor Immigrant"
Published:
10th September, 2019
Autobiography Book 1:
0 – 12 years old

"Poems for Misfits, Miscreants, Misanthropes, Mavericks, Losers & Malcontents!"
Published:
10th June, 2020
Book of Poems 1

"Poems for Troubled Minds & Trouble Hearts"
Published:
10th August, 2020

Book of Poems 2

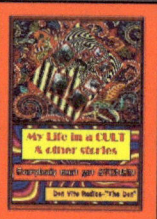
"My Life in a CULT & other stories: Everybody Must Get STONED!"
Published:
10th September, 2020
Autobiography Book 2:
15 – 30 years old

"Poems for Restless Minds & Restless Hearts"
Published:
10th October, 2020
Book of Poems 3

"Poems for Anarchists, Revolutionaries, Outlaws & Dissidents!"
Published:
10th November, 2020

Book of Poems 4

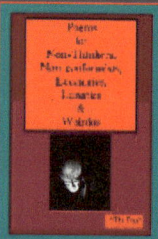
"Poems for Non-Thinkers & Eccentrics"
Published:
10th December, 2020
Book of Poems 5

"The Rantings of a Madman"
Published:
10th January, 2021

Book of Poems 6

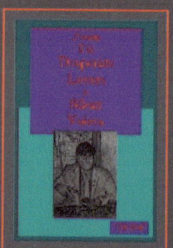
"Poems for Desperate Lovers & Silent Voices"
Published:
10th February, 2021
Book of Poems 7

"Poems for Tormented Minds & Tortured Souls"
Published:
10th March, 2021
Book of Poems 8

All available ONLY online

Books written by "The Don"

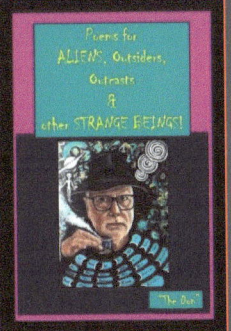

"Poems for ALIENS, Outsiders, Outcasts & other STRANGE BEINGS!"
Published: 10th April, 2021
Book of Poems 9

"Poems for Beings From Another Planet"
Published: 10th May, 2021
Book of Poems 10

"Poems for Mindless Beings & Lost Souls"
Published: 10th June, 2021
Book of Poems 11

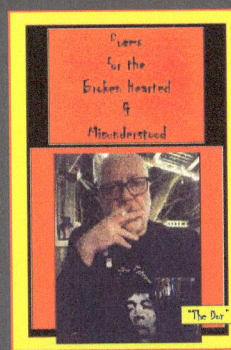

"Poems for the Broken Hearted & Misunderstood
Published: 10th July, 2021
Book of Poems 12

"Poems for Poems for the Bewildered, Dazed & Confused"
10th August, 2021

Book of Poems 13

"Poems for the Outsiders, Displaced, Dispossessed, Discarded & Unwanted"
Published: 10th Sept, 2021
Book of Poems 14

All available ONLY online

"Poems for Secret Agents, Phantom Agents, Agents of Change, Agent Provocateurs & Agents of Chaos"
Published: 10th Oct, 2021
Book of Poems 15

"Poems for Disenchanted, Disillusioned & Delusional"
Published: 10th November, 2021
Book of Poems 16

Books written by "The Don"

"Poems for the Stoners, drugos, ACID takers & Psychedelic LO♥ERS (Everybody Must Get Stoned)"
Published: 10th December, 2021
Book of Poems 17

"Poems for Anarchists, Rebels & Revolutionaries
Published: 10th January, 2022
Book of Poems 18

"Poems for Rebels, Radicals & Revolutionaries (Viva la Révolution!)"
Published: 10th February, 2022
Book of Poems 19

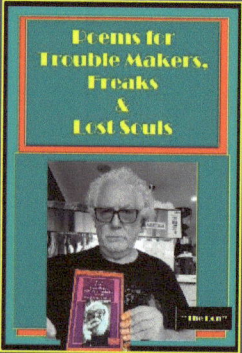

"Poems for Trouble Makers, Freaks & Lost Souls"
Published: 10th March 2022
Book of Poems 20

"Poems for Zombies & the Walking Dead"
Published: 10th April 2022
Book of Poems 21

"Poems for Non-Conformists (Never conform!)"
Published: 10th May 2022
Book of Poems 22

**Vito Radice
("The Don")**
(Poet/Author/Polemicist/Non-Thinker/Non-Intellectual)
Email: vitoradice@gmail.com
Instagram: don_vito_radice
Facebook: Vito Radice
Mobile: +61490012461 (Australia)

www.ingramcontent.com/pod-product-compliance
Lightning Source LLC
Chambersburg PA
CBHW042049290426
44109CB00006B/155